This one is for Lulu Gelonesi, with love – A.G.

For my dancing sisters, Moya, Christine and Tricia – S.McN.

ORCHARD BOOKS
First published in Great Britain in 2011 by Orchard Books
This edition published in 2012 by The Watts Publishing Group

5 7 9 10 8 6 4
Text © Adéle Geras, 2011
Illustrations © Shelagh McNicholas, 2011
The moral rights of the author and illustrator have been asserted.

A CIP catalogue record for this book is available from the British Library.

ISBN 978 1 40830 980 3

Printed and bound in China

Orchard Books
An imprint of Hachette Children's Group
Part of The Watts Publishing Group Limited
Carmelite House
50 Victoria Embankment
London EC4Y 0DZ

An Hachette UK Company
www.hachette.co.uk
www.hachettechildrens.co.uk

My Ballet Dream

Written by Adèle Geras
Illustrated by Shelagh McNicholas

ORCHARD

Everyone calls me Tutu Tilly because I love ballet SO much. I've been going to class for a whole year and now it's time for our big show – the recital!

All the big girls at the dance studio will be in the recital, too.

But my class is going to be baby swans.

We've been practising our steps for ages.

The hardest bit is keeping in time with everyone else.

Today's the day of our dress rehearsal, when we get to dance in our proper costumes. They've been ordered from a real costume shop. We're going to be wearing pink tutus and ballet shoes with satin ribbons. I can't wait to see them!

I'm jumping up and down because I'm so excited.
Mum says I'm more like a little kangaroo than a
baby swan!

Miss Anne is waiting for us in the dressing room . . .

Oh, no! The tutus and shoes are blue!

"I'm afraid they sent the wrong colour," Miss Anne says.
"But never mind, you'll all dance just as well in blue, won't you?
Of course you will!"

I don't think I'll dance nearly as well in blue.

"Cheer up, everyone," says Miss Anne. "Let's get ready, shall we?"

Tying the ribbons on the shoes is very hard.
Mine get tangled and Miss Anne has to help.

I still like twirling round in
my proper ballerina shoes,
even if they are blue!

Next, the mums help with our hair and make-up – lovely pink lipstick, glittery stuff on our eyes and cheeks and butterfly clips for our hair.

Then we stand at the side of the stage and watch the big girls dancing. They're just like real ballerinas and don't seem a bit scared.

But I *am* scared. What if something goes wrong?
What if we don't remember our steps? What if
someone falls over? What will we do?

Lots of things go wrong . . .
First, the pianist plays the wrong tune.
We have to go back and start again.

Bella trips over, so we
have to go back and
start again, AGAIN.

Then, in the middle of the dance,
the ribbons on one of my ballet
shoes come undone . . .
What shall I do?

The music stops and Miss Anne runs over to help me.

"Don't worry, Tilly," she says. "Things often go wrong at dress rehearsals, that's what they're for. You'll be fine tomorrow, after a good night's sleep."

That night, I go to bed and dream of swans
and ribbons and pretty butterflies.

When I wake up, it's the day of the recital! Before I know it, I'm dressed, my ribbons are tied, my hair is done and I feel ready to be a baby swan. I even like my blue tutu!

It's nearly time for our dance and Mum has gone to sit in the
audience with Miss Anne while we wait in the wings . . .

That's our music! It's too late to be nervous. We start dancing.
I can't see Mum or Miss Anne because the lights are so bright.
I count the steps in my head and think all the time,
'I'm a baby swan! I'm a baby swan!'

The music ends. We've done it and we didn't even make a single mistake. The others curtsey, but I forget because there's so much clapping!

Everyone loved our dance! Then it's time to leave the stage, but what about my curtsey?

Well, I run back on to the stage and do my best curtsey ever.
Everyone claps all over again, just for me. It's like a dream!
I can't wait to be in another ballet recital because
I am Tutu Tilly!